EMOTIONALLY ABSENT FATHER:

How to Recognize and Overcome the Effects of Childhood Emotional Neglect

By

Willie G. Taylor

Table of Contents

<u>Chapter 6</u>

<u>Step-by-step instructions to pardon your dad for genuinely Absent</u>

Chapter 1

What is Emotional Absent Father

The capability that a dad plays in a youngster's life is essential to their personality development. A dad's contribution to a kid's life from birth to immaturity and into youthful adulthood shapes how youngster sees themselves and their general surroundings.

This mindfulness and world point of view are molded by direct demonstrations and circuitous connections that the dad has with the youngster. Sincerely missing fathers impact their kids in various ways. These men for the most part esteem monetary things, others, and their work over their kids.

They keep away from profound exchanges with their kids and don't offer a solid climate for their youngsters to convey feelings. They frequently keep or reject love, approval, and good regard leaving their youngsters with unsettled sentiments themselves.

Relationally stunted fathers in some cases come from ages of fathers who are something similar. Relationally stunted fathers who were raised by heavy drinkers have additionally been demonstrated to need close-to-home development in adulthood.

Moreover, survivors of kid misuse, sexual maltreatment, and horrible young lives could frequently endure with close to home accessibility with their kids. While these shared traits exist behind the scenes, they ought not to be used as reasons. They are not the weight of the youngster but rather tragically much of the time repeated in family cycles without help.

One technique to battle the rehashing of these negative family cycle designs is to look for proficient assistance. Through individual treatment, the youngster might figure out how to separate their dad's demonstrations from their own healthy identity. Through this cycle, adolescents will come to discover that their self-esteem isn't anticipated by any demonstrations or inactions of their dad.

They can make self-righteousness through self-talk or getting to male good examples that are beyond their home. This might be through a method for a stepfather, granddad, uncle, educator, guide, or mentor. The main thing for offspring of depressed fathers is to perceive the activities they show and decide whether there is a readiness for the dad to change.

The Impacts of Being Raised by Relationally stunted Guardians

The feeling is the language we use to associate with each other. We could impart straightforwardly utilizing both verbal and non-verbal communication pieces of information. In any case, enthusiasm drives how these experiences are seen. We, at last, collaborate utilizing the utilization of our profound jargon.

We achieve this through aiding each other meet our feelings, yet in addition, using sympathizing with those requirements assuming we can't help them at the time. This is the idea of making oneself sincerely open in a relationship.

Nonetheless, we just foster these capacities from the models given to us by our folks/watchmen. We want positive good examples to give the reference focus to cooperating with others in valid sympathy.

Furthermore, consequently, being raised by sincerely missing guardians generally prompts internal injury that arises as powerlessness to be genuinely present with others. It leads not exclusively to being not able to perceive your necessities, yet in addition, produces an absence of capacity in sympathizing with others.

Side effects Of Being Raised By Depressed Father

Being raised by a sincerely missing guardian or watchman might prompt an existence of unsound fellowships, chains of ineffective connections, profound destitution, powerlessness to self-manage, care for oneself, and character vulnerability. This may likewise produce essential injury encompassing not having the option to convey your needs. At the point when there's been disregard of feelings in early life, it's known as formative injury, which might prompt long-haul repercussions while perhaps not suitably treated.

A portion of these side effects include:

- Rigidity\sLow-Stress Resilience
- Profound Unsteadiness with Hostility
- Unfortunate Limits
- Temperamental Connections

Consideration Seeking\sLong-Term Impacts Of Being Raised By Relationally stunted Guardians On Youngsters

At the point when there's been a deficiency of care through basic consideration suppliers or guardians not being sincerely present, it might fabricate broken thought processes that could produce psychological well-being issues and a failure to interface with individuals later on in adulthood. Some of them incorporate, however, aren't restricted to:

Useless Connections in Adulthood: We model our relationship and correspondence styles on the models we grew up with in adolescence. It's generally present for us and turns into our default method of relating until we decide to fix our programming and make our way of thinking about how to relate.

In any case, it's critical to take note that not all kids with relationally stunted guardians experience unsteady connections in adulthood. It's generally expected, yet not outright.

Separation anxiety in Affection: If there's been a deficiency of affection and warmth during the formative phases of development because of sincerely disengaged guardians, it can prompt kids to turn out to be genuinely removed in their high school years. They could battle to communicate their thoughts genuinely and show love to others since they haven't played sufficient parts models to show them it's alright to be expressive and open with others, inwardly.

Marginal Character and Self-absorbed Attributes: It very well may be the situation - however not dependably - that those raised by genuinely chilly guardians are exposed to egotistical and additionally marginal qualities. Both of these problems make associating with others very troublesome. The conceited, self-important style of the egotistical can cause youngsters to feel alienated from their folks, while BPD qualities can prompt continuous contentions, due to the close-to-home eruptions that can likewise prompt verbal or actual animosity.

Childishness: This can appear in various ways. The sincerely void parent could see their requirements as fundamentally important. In any case, it can likewise be that they could force rules, lines, and limits on their kid to keep them from getting a charge out of something they never had when they were growing up. As most relationally repressed guardians themselves are survivors of their childhood, they'll carry their projections into the relationship with their posterity.

Substance Misuse and Reliance: As the offspring of a sincerely far-off parent enters adulthood, another arrangement of decisions become accessible. By this point, they'll be in such a lot of agony and misery through not having had their feelings met, it can prompt the utilization of sporting or potentially prescriptive medications. This can then begin a pattern of habit-based issues that will frequently go on until the center wound(s) of profound disregard are tended to.

Absence of Character and Heading: One of the central issues confronting numerous grown-ups who endure a childhood from sincerely far-off guardians is the possibility of personality. Since there's been an absence of any genuine fundamental beliefs, all in all, nothing remains to be moored into as a genuinely trustworthy, ethical code or feeling. This outcome in there is no outline for future connections. Thus, those good examples should be tracked down somewhere else in a proxy organization to compensate for the absence of close-to-home direction during the formative phase of development.

Loss of Trust, Confidence, and Euphoria: Perhaps the most unsettling thing that can happen to a sincerely far-off kid's childhood is losing all expectations. Since their folks haven't had the option to articulate their thoughts inwardly, there's frequently been a gigantic shortfall of help. This can be particularly hard when you feel the deficiency of the parent who's still actually present, yet is sincerely stifled so much that it's difficult to associate with them in any significant manner.

Indications Of Relationally stunted Guardians

- They don't pay attention to you
- They don't get some information about your life
- They don't approve/praise your accomplishments
- They aren't willing to participate in exercises with you
- They never offer commendations
- They never burn through alone/one-on-one time with you
- They center around their bliss more than yours
- They can't communicate that they love you

- They can't show you any fondness

Signs Your Folks Were Relationally stunted

There is not a solitary manner by which guardians can be dispassionately inaccessible. Similarly, as with all circumstances inside the scene of psychological wellness, there are numerous articulations that each have their range of force. Here is a portion of the central topics.

Profound Distance

Guardians can't or able to communicate sympathy or profound mindfulness toward their kid

Guardians can't or able to hold space for the profound weakness of their youngster

Guardians can't or are ready to offer their kid consideration except for sickness/crisis

Close to home Precariousness

Guardians are inclined to episodes of blowing up to minor mix-ups/burdens

Guardians can be volatile - in some cases being fair and kind, at different times being nonsensical

Guardians can be irate or opposing towards their youngsters amid close-to-home misery

Mental Rigidity

Guardians can be cautious and reluctant to acknowledge various perspectives other than their own

Guardians can be reluctant to acknowledge realities that go against their viewpoints

Guardians can be reluctant to self-reflect/introspect - or to check out the effect of their activities

Guardians can be extremely unbending and established in highly contrasting reasoning - unfit to acknowledge groundbreaking thoughts

Self-Centredness

Guardians might involve their youngster as a comrade, yet will most likely be unable to satisfy that job for their kid

Guardians will frequently say and get things done without contemplating other's sentiments

Guardians might design discussions to rotate generally around their inclinations

Guardians might overlook or not recognize the outcome of their kid prompting negation

Kinds Of Depressed/Juvenile Guardians

There isn't only one kind of depressed/juvenile parent. In truth, it's difficult to completely sort them into a gathering of models, as there are continuously going to be a few get over between the various arrangements of ways of behaving. In any case, the accompanying model gives a strong establishment to have the option to distinguish what sort of relationally repressed parent you could have been raised by and attempt to mend from now.

The Profound Parent

This is an articulation that is generally established in sensations of close to-home flimsiness that outcomes from a feeling of continuous tension and apprehension for the people who need to cooperate with them. Their temperaments can be significantly increased further by being set off by both people around them and the general difficulties of life. This type can be exceptionally hasty.

The Determined Parent The determined parent is in a steady state of ceaseless movement, attempting to cause everything and everybody to adjust to their guidelines. They are predisposed to anticipate and imprint their conviction system(s) on others through exhortation, and accepting their direction is the primary method.They could have all the earmarks of being strong and making progress, but will attempt to push their own thoughts as an approach to attempting to live vicariously through their kids because of their own childhood.

The Detached Parent This parent can be considered to have an avoidant connection style. They'll attempt to evade a conflict no matter what and manage horrendous feelings. On the other hand, they can be available from a fun-loving perspective.

However, with regards to offering profound help, they can pull out and neglect to hold space for their kids' issues. Inactive guardians are additionally inclined to giving affection to make themselves feel needed and to satisfy their own feelings.

The Dismissing Guardian The dismissing type is one of the most grating of all sincerely youthful guardians. Furthermore, their way of behaving can truly hurt their youngsters, bringing about a great deal of emotional injury. They're inclined to being removed, cavalier, stooping and opposing. They'll transparently dismiss their youngsters' longing for consideration and warmth.

This demeanor causes them to seem to have areas of strength but actually have obstructions, which can likewise cause them to feel both scared and standoffish. In addition, in outrageous cases of this type, this type can likewise be genuinely harmful.

How Would You Respond to Sincere Juvenile Guardians? There are two fundamental responses to sincerely juvenile guardians, contingent upon the character of the kid. These are integrating and externalizing.

In basic terms, this implies that when things turn out badly, externalisers will put others through what's happening, while internalisers will regularly put themselves through what's happening. However, because this model of mental handling operates on a range rather than a dualistic model, you may encounter blended reactions.

Guardians who are depressedOppressive Connections: Since somebody raised by a relationally stunted parent doesn't have the reference point for what a solid relationship resembles, they can fall into examples of useless relationships where they're both the victimizer and the person in question, contingent upon their childhood and their ability to recuperate from their disregard.

As the needs of a grown-up overcomer of depressed guardians have been neglected for such a long time as a kid-as well as being dismissed when requested-there may be an instance of not feeling like their necessities will be met in adulthood. This frequently prompts withdrawal, downgrading, and not having the option to request that others regard their limits.

Poverty: This can be another huge block. Because the needs of the child have been neglected for so long, the grown-up overcomer of truly separated guardians is effectively barred from consideration and warmth.This can prompt overcompensating, as they look to get their necessities met, which have never been met, making their relationship elements extremely lopsided and frequently undesirable.

Being raised by genuinely missing/youthful guardians can likewise seed relational issues like restless connection, avoidant connection, and unfortunate avoidance (scattered connection).

Codependency: This can be one more typical example, as there's been no truly parental figure to display positive ways of behaving during the formative years, there might be a feeling of projection onto future companions and accomplices, which can prompt the further disintegration of limits.

Many children of relationally repressed parents will likewise rely on human satisfying to meet their needs.Since they've been kept from their center requirements for such a long time, they'll, in a real sense, successfully make up for the shortcoming left by their childhood.

One more way individuals raised by sincerely disengaged parents find they can get a portion of their requirements met is through sex. This can cause habitual inclinations, which makes them inclined toward momentary delight since they never know when their requirements will be met in the future. This steady search for quickness can likewise prompt dependence on sex.

Desire and Possessiveness: This can be cultivated in both non-romantic and heartfelt connections. When the offspring of relationally stunted parents finally form a relationship with someone in adulthood who appears to be stable, they may be reluctant to abandon that individual, motivated by a paranoid fear of being abandoned.

There can likewise be a feeling of value that stems from never getting satisfactory consideration or warmth from genuinely segregated and far-off guardians. On the off chance that affection has never been gotten during formative years, that makes the example of being repulsive, which extraordinarily influences confidence.

How Would You Manage Relationally Stunned Guardians? At first, a comprehension of your circumstance is expected to secure that you're really a casualty of circumstance and the treatment/non-treatment you got from your folks isn't your shortcoming. It's critical to disconnect from the mold of disgrace around being loathsome or undesirable. So, from that point, you view what is happening from a more objective perspective without the charge of your own feelings hindering you from seeing the reason why you were dealt with-and are as yet treated-how you are.

The following stage is design acknowledgment, which requires knowing your parent's style of correspondence and limit. When you can moor in their absence of presence is because of their absence of limit because of their own injury, it turns out to be a lot simpler to explore the relationship and discover a feeling of conclusion. Acquiring this understanding of your parent's circumstance, while not something you can do in adolescence, turns out to be a lot more straightforward to achieve as a component of a helpful mending process later on in adulthood. It's not your problem that you did not see this in adolescence.

The way to managing and recuperating from a childhood from sincerely far-off guardians is to be available with what's being shared. Furthermore, you may experience a lamenting cycle as you realize your parent(s) will never be able to guide and coach you in the manner you require. Yet, what's more regrettable than this is living under the assumption that you can transform them. Sadly, you can't-and shouldn't have any desire to-change others. Yet, you can change your view of them by understanding their story and how it illuminates their activities. That is also the pith of the recuperating system.

Chapter 2

Role of a Father in Child Development?

Fathers assume a significant part in the turn of events and development of their youngsters.

An elaborate dad advances inward development and strength.

Research shows that the affection and care of fathers are similarly significant for the physical and psychological well-being, and prosperity of a kid however much a mother's affection is significant.

The two dads and moms are similarly significant. Fathers have feelings. They do mind, cry, get injured, and love bounteously.

A dad's presence is gotten and steady too. Anybody can parent a kid yet being a father takes a lifetime, a protective pretends an extremely significant job in each youngster's life and that can't be filled by any other person.

While society frequently lays out the image of a dad as the sole provider and the mother as the sole guardian for the kids, a youngster should have both dad and mother assume a part in their general turn of events. While mothers are normally the ones who assume responsibility for the childhood of the youngster as they are sustaining, a dad plays a vital part to play if he believes his kid should develop into an even grown-up.

Fathers very much like moms are the mainstay of profound improvement of a kid's prosperity and thinking. Kids admire their dads to set out the guidelines and implement them they, likewise admire their dads to give a sense that everything is good, actual security and profound security. They likewise admire their dads as good examples so the mental and social improvement of a kid must be guaranteed well while a dad is near.

At the point when I was at an eligible age and my folks caused me to sit one day with them and we were simply talking and they requested me what sort of fellow do you like, what kind of man do you like in your life, and quickly I said very much like daddy, why since all the basic reassurance as a little girl I needed from my dad I have, all the consolation, all the security, monetary, actual security, consistently we have been informed that whatever happens-no matter what I'm there and that matters a great deal to a little girl, he has been a caring dad, a delicate dad, and that precisely what we looking for in the individual I plan to wed.

And keeping in mind that I am talking according to the viewpoint of a girl, children are likewise admiring their dad as it were. I have a 10-year-old child, and I see him contrasting and my significant other, attempting to spruce up like him, attempting to talk like his dad, attempting to safeguard me - his mother, reflecting very much like my better half does. He attempts to act like a grown-up very much like my better half is acting with his sister.

This is the kind of thing my kid is attempting to emulate, duplicate and gain from his dad, he expects that while he looks for all the profound love and embraces and contacts from me, he guarantees that he gets constantly, the innocent games, the innocent discussions from my significant other and my better half is there to give him, so when I'm talking according to a girls point of view or a children viewpoint, a dad is vital.

Frequently I have seen my little one letting me know I'm hanging around for you when his father is voyaging, that makes me grin as someplace he is excessively youthful to comprehend that his mom is similarly skilled however as far as he might be concerned, his dad is solid, cherishing, compassionate, major areas of strength for genuinely he figures out him

To every one of the dads, it is vital that even while your soul mate is pregnant, you are there with your significant other, you guarantee that you give that touch to the kid while the kid is in the belly, you give all the adoration and backing to your significant other because recall, the affection and regard you look for from your kid when the kid is out on the planet, it's the precisely exact thing you want to provide for your kid in the belly.

That is the motivation behind why we have moved forward, there is maternity leave and paternity leave since society presently needs them. Fathers were less dynamic assuming that we think back in the set of experiences, in joint family framework kids were raised by ladies.

Today the circumstance has changed. There are more family units, and more modest families which is the explanation representatives are getting paternity leave. So that fathers get the potential chance to engage in the process from the time, a kid is conceived. Additionally, in every one of the classes, they take during pregnancy why is supported that couple partakes together so you are holding and understanding the entire normal interaction together? Nurturing liability is similarly shared and taken an interest and fathers these days are available at the hour of labor - it shows that we are changing and developing, and nurturing is continually evolving. Fathers are e now more inquisitive and extremely involved too, from diaper changing to taking care of to going to a ball game are the jobs fathers are likewise fit for doing and fathers are doing that too. I feel it is uncalled for to say that they are deciding not to do and I generally express that to be reasonable for the dads who don't partake I think some of the time it is simply passed on to be accepted that we want assistance, particularly moms and not conveyed. Whenever imparted, things are without a doubt better.

Nurturing isn't a contest, moms likewise need to support more dynamic cooperation and positively and she likewise needs to at times step back and leave kids alone with their dads. Have some spa time or shopping time with your companions and let the daddy dear be there with the children and plan their trip.

Significance of a Dad in a Youngster's Life

The youngsters with involved fathers are probably going to be more sure, sincerely secure, and frame better friendly bonds. Their instructive results are much of the time better compared to kids with fathers who are less involved, and they are bound to have better relational abilities and better educated working. The significance of a dad in a kid's improvement is unquestionable as youngsters can figure out how to all the more likely direct their way of behaving during the perky and invigorating exercises a dad is bound to give.

What Is the Job of a Dad in Youngster Improvement?

Here we take a gander at the fundamental justifications for why a dad really should be engaged with the improvement of a youngster:

1. Defender

An Elaborate dad gives his youngster a sense of safety, whether physical, profound, mental or otherworldly. At the point when a kid knows, their dad will show up for him regardless of what the circumstance is, it works in them a feeling of certainty, security, and strength that can never be supplanted.

2. Teacher

As the top of the family, a dad should show his kids the fundamental standards and values for them to continue in their lives. A dad must train his kids about the set of principles that should be followed while living in the general public, likewise how to confront the world and he should help them to be focused, polite and conscious. With a dad assuming his part well, a kid will be more propelled to continue to chip away at themselves.

3. Good example

Guardians are continuously being watched by their kids, seeing what they do and how they treat others. A dad is a significant good example for his kids as they will gain what a man ought to be from his model. His children will mirror his way of behaving and form into men with comparable qualities as their dads, and the young ladies will likewise involve their dads as good examples, frequently looking for similar attributes he showed in the mate that they search out when they are mature enough. Fathers should continuously demonstrate acceptable conduct for their youngsters with the goal that their children grow up kind, conscious and noteworthy towards individuals around them. Little girls will want to comprehend that a man ought to be thoughtful, delicate, and minding towards his ladies, yet solid and ready to safeguard them.

4. Companion

Framing a solid relationship with your kid will make way for you two to become companions as grown-ups. However, it is dependably critical to ensure that you put down stopping points so your kids don't exploit you, having a nearby and well-disposed relationship with your kids will make them less inclined to wander from the correct way and fall into unwanted propensities. Kids will be less inclined to become discouraged, and it is simpler to direct your kids when they are agreeable around you.

5. Performer

Fathers are all the more frequently the ones who are more engaged with goofing off with the youngsters. They are more ready to stay aware of their children during play as it is burdening on the body. An elaborate dad will appreciate having his youngsters ride around on his back, play get, and do other proactive tasks that can at times be demanding. He can frequently train them to take care of issues during play and structure procedures during play. Playing with kids will assist them with turning out to be more adaptable, and fit, form their muscles and foster better dexterity. That, yet youngsters will likewise figure out how to keep the guidelines and to be a decent game during recess. All of this frequently assists them with framing bonds with one another.

6. Instructor

A dad shouldn't just be a companion and performer however ought to likewise have the option to direct his kids on the off chance that they at any point need it. This is particularly significant for young men, and when young ladies become confounded regarding the reason why young men act a specific way, having their dads there to make sense of things for them will assist them with filling in their personality and understanding. Your kids ought to be open about their concerns or challenges so make a point to open dependent upon them about your own life as a youngster and the illustrations you learned while growing up.

Assist them with tackling their concerns with responsiveness and certainty, be they school-related or individual matters. Train them on the correct method for dealing with a tough spot and permit them to realize that you are there for them, regardless of whether nothing remains at this point but to embrace them.

All of this will assist them with figuring out how to tackle their concerns and will assume an immense part in their close-to-home, mental and otherworldly turn of events.

7. Coach

Be the holistic mentor that your kids need and show them the significant fundamental abilities that they will require when they are beginning to track down their spot on the planet. Train them to ride bicycles, how fix their messed-up toys, how make things, and how swim.

There are so many different things that a dad can show his kids. Your kids will seek you for direction and will pause and strive to procure your endorsement. Be empowering and steady and offer them a lot of chances to procure your commendation.

8. Accomplice

Being a decent accomplice to your better half is a generally excellent guide to set for your youngsters and something frequently neglected. Not exclusively can they see how a man and lady can cooperate to make solidarity and concordance in the home, yet they will profit from filling in such a climate. In homes where both the guardians are not engaged with the childhood of the kids, the equilibrium is typically disturbed, and the youngsters will become inclined to coerce, uneasiness and stress, which will frequently make them have a chronic weakness.

People are not something similar, and every one of them plays their part to play in the childhood of youngsters. For this reason, it is frequently truly challenging for single guardians to step into the job of the two guardians. The methodologies that people have towards nurturing are unique, however, cooperating can be something excellent for your youngster. While moms might be more careful of their youngsters, fathers will quite often permit and even urge their kids to face solid challenges that will help in their development and improvement. So don't avoid connecting more with your kids; not exclusively will you help them develop and form into even grown-ups, but you will make recollections together that you and the children will hold profoundly in your souls for your entire lives.

Chapter 3

Reasons for irresponsible Father

A Decree to the World educates, "Guardians have a consecrated obligation to raise their kids in adoration and uprightness... By divine plan, fathers are to direct their families in affection and honesty and are dependable to give the necessities of life and security for their families." There are critical adverse consequences when these obligations are dismissed by missing dads.

Fathers bring more to the table than an additional proportion of testosterone under the rooftop. At the point when a dad decides to be a solid figure, this conveys to his youngster that they can investigate with, play with, talk with, and rely upon him to add to their sound development.Child is bound to do well-communicating feelings solidly, foster a solid connection that prompts elevated confidence, and prevail in school scholastically when the dad is available and reliable.Specialists have found these good results stream into the kid's adulthood as they enter the labor force as well.

The job of a dad isn't only fundamental for youngsters, yet in addition for the mother. At the point when just the mother is free, their life becomes consumed with really focusing on the youngsters. This additional pressure can prompt undesirable nurturing rehearses and burnout. By having the two guardians present, jobs can be better settled while as yet taking into account independence to chip away at individual qualities and ambitions.

What is the explanation these dads are not remaining near?

However just having kids can recommend being a dad, for some men, there is more a dad needs to accommodate their loved ones. Joblessness and absence of instruction can be contributing variables concerning why fathers leave.When men feel they are not fulfilling the social needs that characterize fathers, accomplishing other caring jobs diminishes and it might appear to be more straightforward to leave. Different explanations behind the father's nonattendance can incorporate detainment, disloyalty, and misuse.

The most effective method to Help Offspring of Missing Dads

However the adverse results of father nonappearance can dampen, there is still expect these youngsters.

Incorporate positive expanded male family figures in the youngster's life. Youngsters can have areas of strength for shape as they have a protected, stable male figure to depend upon as they develop up.

This could emerge out of a grandparent, uncle, or another positive male relative. At the point when these men are available for stupendous minutes throughout everyday life, as well as everyday communications, a void can be filled, and the youngster's certainty can grow.

Including a more distant family can likewise give one more asset to the mother to assist with lessening pressure over-burden and sensations of dejection.

On the off chance that there is no male relative accessible or close to help, take a stab at tracking down a guide locally. At the point when a kid can invest energy with an effective person locally, various entryways of potential are opened to them to see ways that they can become successful.

Instances of tutors could be mentors, educators, after-school staff, ministerial pioneers, and so on.

Find support bunches in the neighborhood. Very much like youngsters can find guides, single parents can find others dealing with these difficulties.

There genuinely is strength in numbers. Conceptualize, organize, and help one another. However the past may not change, but the future direction can be a positive one. Set aside a few minutes for you.

Growing up without a dad brings gambles, however, that doesn't decide you or your kid's future. Bastard families can become strong in their situation. Let the individuals who your youngster will communicate with know about their battles. Educators, overseers, and other local area figures can assist with reducing the troubles your kid might confront. Yet, they can't help on the off chance that they don't know. Keep in mind, that there is potential for more splendid days to come. Some fathers decided to remain in their youngster's life after growing up without their dads. You don't need to allow the truant to figure out what your family will turn into.

"We want fathers to understand that obligation doesn't end at origination. We want them to understand that what makes you a man isn't the capacity to have a kid - it's the boldness to raise one."- President Barack Obama

I know such countless dads who were scarcely present when their kids were growing up. However, the dad's job is a most significant one since, besides giving a protected home, he should complete the obligations of parenthood perseveringly.

That incorporates cherishing backing, direction, and support in winning life's fights.

The following are things a dependable dad won't ever do.

1. He won't ever set a terrible model.

How frequently have you heard a dad let his children know that there are sure things they should not do, such as blowing their top and acting seriously? The issue is that a few dads lose it and are not a good example for their children by any means. They blow their top while driving and revile different drivers boisterously. They fail to remember that children duplicate ways of behaving.

"Each father ought to recollect that one day his child will follow his model rather than his recommendation." - Charles F. Kettering.

2. He won't ever beat or hit his children.

A reckless dad utilizes actual brutality and beating to force the principles. Yet, a decent stickler knows how to utilize different strategies which are undeniably more compelling in the long haul. Utilizing brutality is showing a youngster that hostility is one approach to managing struggle.

3. He won't ever drop ideal time with his children.

Youngsters anticipate that guardians should be available. Obsessive worker fathers never cut out the opportunity to be with their children and they feel ignored and deserted. Getting a charge out of games, motion pictures and excursions together is valuable and a great dad knows that and will seldom drop due to some earnest work responsibility.

4. He will always remember significant achievements.

Fathers need to recall the achievements in their children's lives and promise to be there. These can be anything from a significant match to a birthday celebration or graduation from secondary school. The most ideal way to get to realize a youngster all around well is by following his advancement and accomplishments. At the point when fathers neglect to turn up, kids are truly frustrated.

"A savvy father knows his kid."- William Shakespeare

5. He won't ever reprimand his children unjustifiably.

You know the scene. Fathers will quite often pick openings and censure their children's endeavors and put down them. They don't understand that when a youngster washes the vehicle, they need to support them by lauding them for working effectively. Assuming they have missed a few filthy spots, the capable dad lets his children know that they ought to go over the vehicle and check for the more modest spots they might have missed. It is likewise an approach to training children to finish the work well.

At the point when I let my dad know that I was giving my all, his answer was "Your best isn't adequate!' It was exceptionally deterring.

6. He won't ever let his relationship with his companion influence how he treats his children.

At the point when struggle and strain start to sharpen relationships, kids are much of the time the first to endure. A heartless and unfeeling dad will allow his hatred to dominate and may well invest less energy with the children as an approach to settling the score with his better half or accomplice. A capable dad will constantly allow his valuable qualities to rule everyday life.

7. He won't ever show slightly.

At the point when a dad loves and regards his companion and children, this establishes the vibe for family connections. In any case, when a dad permits discourtesy and harshness to prosper and never conceals this from his children, they will always be unable to cherish and regard him. This ought to be proportional and it is a fundamental component of dependable parenthood.

8. He won't ever be a dictator.

Most nurturing specialists bring up the distinction between being a tyrant and legitimate. The previous implies that the dad is in every case right and forces the standards in an extremely cruel and frequently savage way. Being legitimate implies that the dad will offer his children decisions and opportunities to fill in a warm and strong climate. You can peruse more about this in Laurence Steinberg's book called We Know A few Things: Juvenile parent Connections By and large and Prospect.

9. He won't ever be lenient.

The opposite finish of the range is where fathers permit their children free rein to do what they like and they completely ruin them. This is unreliable because this present reality out there is loaded with hindrances, cutoff points, and rules. Being lenient is the absolute worst way you can raise a kid since the person in question won't ever work well in the public eye.

"Individuals are saying it takes a town to bring up a kid, yet first it takes a mother and a dad, who are understanding, caring, sustaining, and capable - cooperating to impart discipline, character, trustworthiness, and obligation in their youngsters."- Charles Ballard

10. He won't ever be segregated.

Flighty dads put their youngsters at extensive gambling. They reject or can't be tried to care for them while playing or when they need basic encouragement. The such separation will undoubtedly prompt injury at a physical and mental level. This is the perspective of Anita Gurian who is a teacher at the Kid and Juvenile Psychiatry unit at the NYUMedicalSchool.

11. He won't ever deceive his kids.

"So my dad was an individual who never deceived me. On the off chance that I had an inquiry, he responded to it. I knew a ton of things very early in life since I was fascinated." - Scratch Gun.

Research shows that by the age of 5, kids are master liars! A considerable lot of them have gained workmanship from watching their folks lie. The guardians now and again let them know how to do it by recommending they lie to their grandparents to imagine they like their presents. Another most loved is to request that they let guests know that they are not at home when they are in. There are even guardians who are ready to lie about their residency to get them into a superior school. They risk as long as 20 years in jail if they do that. What an extraordinary model!

It is hence a shock to discover that guardians fly off the handle when their children lie to them. In any case, who educated them? A capable dad or mother will know the risks of lying and will continuously attempt to come clean with them.

12. He won't ever disregard a supplication for help.

At the point when things turn out badly, it is awful on the off chance that your dad isn't there or in any event, ready to tune in. He never possesses any energy for his children. The children feel that they have nobody to go to except if Mother will assist. There is presently much discussion in the UK about changing the Dickensian regulations on disregard of youngsters which were presented in the Victorian time. The proposed regulation would make kid disregard a criminal offense.

13. He won't ever affront his children.

I know a few extremely severe and rather brutal dads who make a propensity for annoying or mocking their children. They call them dumb, lethargic, and messy, just to refer to a couple. There is continuously something to reprimand and they are doing this before companions, family members, and even associates. The capable dad will decide in favor of lauding and empowering their kids with the goal that they never have low confidence.

14. He will love constantly his children.

"I can't consider any need in that frame of mind as the requirement for a dad's security."- Sigmund Freud.

A dependable dad will love constantly his children in any circumstances. In any event, when relationships separate, a dad should constantly keep in touch, regardless of whether he is at the opposite apocalypse. It is so significant for the mother not to demolish or dirty the youngster's perspective on his dad. The equivalent goes for the dad because regularly guardians utilize the miserable occasion to slander the other accomplice. Therefore guardians ought to continuously urge their children to set up a Skype account with the goal that they can in any case keep in touch.

Chapter 4

Recuperating from a Dad Wound

It's nothing unexpected there's a great deal of writing out there on the "mother wound." The harm a mother can have on a youngster when she's genuinely or truly inaccessible is unquestionable. But, the "father wound" isn't discussed sufficiently, taking into account the critical effect it can have on an individual.

You may not perceive the expression "father twisted," yet you presumably know the more famous expression "daddy issues." And keeping in mind that it's generally connected with ladies, men are similarly prone to be affected adversely by their dads. This figure of speech is likewise frequently utilized on TV and in motion pictures to make sense of a person's confounding issues. Models that strike a chord remember Tyrion Lannister for Round of Privileged positions, whose father never acknowledged him for being conceived as a smaller person. Or then again Barney Stinson from How I Met Your Mom, who never met his dad until adulthood. Who these characters are as grown-ups straightforwardly connect with how their dads treated them.

While this injury is an undeniable and moving issue to survive, fortunately recuperating a dad wound is conceivable. The initial step is to comprehend the potential harm a dad wound can cause and why it merits tending to.

What Is a Dad Wound?

"Father wound" is one more term for father truancy. The point when an individual's dad is genuinely missing, sincerely far off or an oppressive, negative, or excessively basic person, can have long haul ramifications for the person. Guardians are the main individual kids figure out how to cherish, so when they're unsupportive in any capacity, it can send a negative message.

Harm Brought about by a Dad Wound

The impacts of a sincerely missing dad can affect a singular's confidence, connections, and, surprisingly, inspiration throughout everyday life.

Low Confidence

A dad wound can impart sensations of not measuring up to assumptions, not being sufficient, and being undeserving of affection. Youngsters don't have the knowledge to comprehend that their folks can have issues, so they will more often than not incorporate their folks' way of behaving as their shortcomings. Low confidence can bring about a person:

Never propelling themselves into the everyday schedule

Experiencing issues opening up and associating with others, making it hard to frame significant, durable connections and kinships

Being more defenseless to substance misuse

Outrage, Discouragement, and Uneasiness

A dad wound can leave an individual inclination low, discouraged or restless about their parental relationship. A parent should offer genuine love, and on the off chance that you see that others have that, it's difficult to comprehend the reason why you don't. Frequently, this tension or misery goes to outrage. People might feel denied of blissful, ordinary youth. They may likewise feel profoundly hurt by their dad's activities or non-appearance and become angry.

Unbending Limits

On the off chance that your dad frequently showed up after the expected time or missed significant occasions in your day-to-day existence, you might overcompensate by defining very unbending limits in adulthood. You might feel everything should be booked and arranged, and you can only with significant effort pardon individuals for being late, dropping, or needing to reschedule. This is an endeavor to recapture a feeling of control you didn't have growing up with a missing dad.

Free Limits

Another chance is the other limit of having free limits. Assuming your dad was excessively basic and never appeared to be content with what you did, you might foster the need to if it's not too much trouble, individuals. You frantically need acknowledgment and endorsement, so you can't say no. Assuming that specific individual in your day-to-day existence notice this way of behaving, they might rush to exploit it.

Unfortunate Decisions in Better halves

Your folks are your most memorable illustration of what a relationship resembles. The vast majority unknowingly try to repeat the relationship dynamic with their folks in their connections in adulthood. Without your acknowledging it, a dad wound might make you look for accomplices who rehash the negative ways of behaving of your dad. This can mean an accomplice who's missing, tyrannical, or excessively basic. We search this out because it brings a feeling of commonality and solace. Notwithstanding, picking an accomplice like your dad just rehashes your injury from youth.

Pattern of Misuse

Sadly, casualties of misuse can now and again proceed with the cycle when they become guardians themselves. On the off chance that you didn't have a strong illustration of good nurturing, being a decent parent yourself is more enthusiastic. You could wind up accidentally rehashing the missteps your dad made. Assuming that somebody has gotten through torment, they need to safeguard their kid from going through a similar encounter. This makes tending to your dad's wound basic for you, however for your partner(s) and your kids.

Step-by-step instructions to Be aware If You Have a Dad Wound

You might have a dad wound if you can distinguish key pointers while pondering your experience growing up. These can incorporate that your dad:

- Was now and again missing
- Was genuinely missing or oppressive
- Was exceptionally reproachful of you and continually objected to your activities, decisions, and ways of behaving
- Kept food, love, or different fundamentals as a type of discipline
- Was harmful

You may likewise review that you frequently felt terrified of your dad or feel your relationship was rarely great and stays rough or nonexistent today.

Instructions to Recuperate From a Dad Wound

As we referenced, mending a dad wound isn't just imaginable yet exceptionally empowered. Resolving these issues can assist you with redressing your sentiments about your experience growing up and give you clearness on a portion of your ways of behaving as a grown-up.

The initial step is to distinguish and acknowledge that you have a dad wound. Then, you'll need to look for proficient treatment to assist you with managing this injury. Your advisor might walk you through survey things through your dad's eyes. Not all fathers merit pardoning, but rather some may. Moreover, your advisor might set you up to defy your dad so you can feel appreciated and make sense of the effect his activities had on your life. From that point, you'll figure out how to separate from a portion of the convictions and ways of behaving you embraced because of your dad's wound. You can then put forth a purposeful attempt to turn into a better variant of yourself and credit how far you've come.

Chapter 5

Childhood Emotional Neglect and Abuse

What Is Childhood Emotionally Neglect

Youth profound disregard is a sort of psychological mistreatment that frequently goes unnoticed and unreported. This type of youngster abuse isn't generally clear since not many individuals discuss it or understand what signs to search for.

Being genuinely disregarded can be a staggering encounter. Not exclusively might this youth injury at any point influence the youngster's identity, their ability to trust, and their capacity to construct solid connections, but it can likewise influence a kid's medical issue. The impacts of mental maltreatment can continue in one's grown-up life.

In the US, youngster disregard incorporates physical, clinical, instructive, and close-to-home disregard

1 . Parental disregard truly hurting through the disavowal of legitimate consideration or the absence of oversight is a crook go about as characterized by Government Youngster Misuse Counteraction and Treatment Act (CAPTA, 1996).

forlorn kid checking out at the downpour outside the window

What Is Youth Close to home Disregard? (Meaning Of Disregard)

Youngster close-to-home disregard (CEN) is the parent's inability to meet their kid's feelings during the early years. It includes inert, inaccessible, and restricted profound connections between that individual and the kid. Youngsters' feelings for friendship, backing, consideration, or capability are disregarded.

CEN likewise happens when the parent or essential guardian opens the youngster to outrageous aggressive behavior at home, permits the kid to take part in maladaptive ways of behaving, will not look for treatment for the kid's issues, or doesn't give them satisfactory design.

Maternal hardship, for example, is regulated or set in a halfway house, which is likewise a type of close-to-home disregard. Offspring of missing guardians may likewise encounter comparative disregard.

the forlorn kid sits on the love seat

Impacts Of Profound Disregard In Adolescence

Youngster profound disregard is a type of mental abuse. It is likewise one of the most predominant kinds of experiences growing up misuse

2. Notwithstanding the absence of unmistakable horrendous mishaps, encountering close-to-home disregard as a youngster can be similarly pretty much as harmful as misuse

3. Truth be told, studies demonstrate that CEN could have the most colossal negative psychological well-being influence among all youth abuse types. It is related to antagonistic physical, mental, and instructive results.

The transient outcomes of disregard incorporate expanded risk for youth incorporating and externalizing conduct, as well as postpones in mental and profound turn of events.

Amygdala is the piece of the cerebrum liable for learning close-to-home importance. It influences excitement response to ecological boosts

At the point when a youngster encounters extreme types of CEN during early mental health, for example, institutional raising, the amygdala expands in volume and more receptive.

Subsequently, people raised by careless guardians will generally have more terrible emotional well-being results and long-haul impacts.

A kid's impression of disregard is significant. At the point when a kid sees they're being ignored inwardly, they are two times as prone to foster mental problems by age 15, including the improvement of misery, bipolar confusion, uneasiness, alarm turmoil, fears, and posttraumatic stress jumble (PTSD). Young people with their feelings ignored as a kid are bound to have unfortunate scholarly execution, substance misuse, hazardous sexual action, and self-destruction endeavors.

Profound disregard is frequently transgenerational

Guardians who have encountered an absence of support in youth from their folks will generally take on comparative nurturing styles while bringing up their youngsters.

kid checks out at the rear of the parent behind the wall

Indications Of Young life Close to home Disregard

Not at all like actual disregard or misuse, careless nurturing doesn't have outward signs like injuries or wounds.

Side effects of profound disregard in a kid are unobtrusive. Regardless of individual contrasts, dismissed individuals will generally show specific standards of conduct.

Likewise, misuse encounters are in many cases joined by different kinds of misuse, for example, actual maltreatment or sexual maltreatment, which will generally have more clear signs.

Indications OF Genuinely Careless FATHER

- Talk with a cold and unpleasant tone
- Inert to the kid's sentiments
- Excuse the kid's feelings
- Try not to converse with the kid definitely
- Invest little energy with the kid and cause them to feel they are undesirable
- More negative criticism or applause
- Express less warmth
- Show more negative social associations
- Withdrawn and uninvolved in the youngster's life
- Indifference toward youngsters' exercises
- Tirelessly see a major problem with their kid
- Overlook the youngster's prompts for help in critical thinking errands

- Offer no support when the kid bombs an undertaking
- Verbally forceful discipline
- Dependent on substance abuse
- Show burdensome side effects
- Experienced close to home disregard themselves in their own young life

Family treatment with prepared emotional well-being experts can help both the careless mother, careless dad, and disregarded youngster. Treatment can assist guardians with figuring out the extreme effect of their disregard. A decent specialist can likewise show the youngster legitimate survival strategies. Through early intercession, ways of behaving that lead to disregard might be changed and revised.

The side effects of life as a youngster disregard, as a rule, improve when dismissed kids are thusly focused on by cherishing relatives, particularly before age two.

Dismissed Guardians

Guardians who had careless early educational encounters themselves can likewise profit from others' consistent encouragement. One review has shown that defeating adolescents profound disregard can be accomplished with parent assistant advising (lay guiding) and Guardians Unknown. These compelling treatment choices have moderately high achievement rates.

NEGLECTED ADULTS

Research demonstrates one out of five people experienced childhood in a family climate where guardians denied them affection and consideration without misuse.

Dismissed grown-ups who have encountered profound relinquishment as a kid are at raised risk of incorporating misery and substance misuse. Getting proficient assistance to address the drawn-out impacts of depressed guardians is particularly significant.

It is normal for grown-ups to try not to look for help. They like to deal with issues all alone. Be that as it may, conquering youth misuse doesn't involve resolution. Indeed, even as grown-ups, manhandled kids can struggle with adapting to a horrendous past. With the assistance of accomplished emotional well-being proficiency, you can accelerate your recuperating interaction.

Youth's profound disregard is not even close as clear as one would envision. In the first place, there's the truth that a kid may not perceive abuse except if it has something to balance it with. As that youngster develops into adulthood, the aftermath of prior disregard can be misidentified. You can wind up battling as a grown-up and not know why.

All of the above can hamper any effort to recuperate. Except if basic causes can be found and settled, encountering a profound recovery is interesting. In this way, it very well may be colossally critical to initially figure out how to perceive when the profound disregard you endured as a kid is popping up.

The Vital Indication of Young life Close to home Disregard

Maybe the most inescapable sign is a feeling of deadness or vacancy. This can affect you in various ways, for example, you experience separation from your sentiments and the sensations of others. Here are a few instances of how this separation might show:

It very well may be a strict actual sensation, for example, a bunch in the stomach or a snugness in their throat.

You feel trouble while endeavoring to observe what individuals anticipate from you regarding social communications and feelings. You additionally may track down it difficult to comprehend the reason why individuals act as they do.

Communicating your sentiments is a significant test with the result of being silenced. You frequently don't have the foggiest idea how you feel, or your feelings are missing

The apprehension about passing up a great opportunity is available however you genuinely don't have any idea what it is you're passing up. This can prompt an insight that you are exceptionally defective.

You're a savagely independent

Other Key Indications of Young life Profound Disregard

Hairsplitting and a significant feeling of dread toward dismissal

Deciding for yourself also cruelly and afterward encountering low confidence

You'll successfully keep away from a feeling of being reliant upon any other person

Never requesting help

Being effectively overwhelmed, You feel ongoing culpability and disgrace

At the point when you're furious, it is typically independent

You're an accommodating person

You effectively point empathy at others — even outsiders — yet are in every case exceptionally unforgiving with yourself

Every individual is unique and it's to be expected for signs and side effects to cover. In any case, significant set forth the energy to look for help while rehearsing however much-taking care of oneself as could reasonably be expected.

Instructions to Begin Mending From Youth Close to home Disregard

1. Acknowledgment

Recognizing misuse or disregard because of a friend or family member can be unbelievably troublesome. However, tolerating that this happened is pivotal for recuperating. Likewise, you should make progress toward tolerating what this youth experience is as yet meaning for you. No disgrace is being impacted by something beyond your control. What is influenced quite a bit by now is getting the assistance you with requiring.

2. Mindfulness

The following stage in the wake of embracing acknowledgment is to expand your mindfulness. As referenced above, youth's profound disregard can bring about casualties moving away from their feelings. This makes it doubly vital to give close consideration to anything you do feel. Your folks and guardians didn't take care of what you felt. This is presently your opportunity to re-parent and nature yourself. A decent specialist can help you reconnect with your profound self.

3. Self-Empathy

A major piece of re-nurturing yourself is learning self-empathy. Indulge yourself with a similar sympathy and compassion you would have for a friend or family member or dear companion. Monitor what you like so you can provide yourself with a consistent stock of that!

How would you adapt to Adolescence Close to home Disregard (CEN)

Growing up with Adolescence Close to home Disregard positions you to battle with a progression of difficulties as a grown-up.

Adolescence Close to home Disregard (CEN) happens when your folks neglect to answer enough to your feelings as they raise you.

At the point when you grow up this way you consequently close your sentiments off as a kid to adapt to the understood messages in your life as a youngster at home.

No Sentiments Permitted.

With your feelings walled off, you go through your pre-adulthood and adulthood lacking full admittance to a strong, indispensable fixing from the inside: your feelings, which ought to be propelling, coordinating, interfacing, invigorating, and enabling you.

At the point when you are experiencing along these lines, it's difficult to see the issue, or even that there is an issue. Most kids in sincerely careless homes have no clue that anybody ought to see their sentiments, approve of them, or answer them. Then, at that point, when they develop into grown-ups, they keep on having no clue.

However, as a grown-up who grew up with Profound Disregard, you most likely may detect that something isn't right with you, yet you don't have the foggiest idea what it is.

When you comprehend that you passed up a critical component of experience growing up, you are at last opened up to fix the issue.

You can offer yourself what you never got — close-to-home consideration and approval — and figure out how to associate with your sentiments and how to utilize them.

Adolescence Close to home Disregard might leave you feeling to some degree unfilled and detached, lost, or alone. Be that as it may, uplifting news! There are strong things you can do to adapt.

Systems For Adapting To Your Life as a youngster Close to home Disregard

1. Profoundly recognize how Close home Disregard occurred in your family and what it's meant for you.

This isn't generally so natural as it would sound. It means quite a bit to attempt to comprehend, for instance, was it one parent or both? Did your folks neglect to answer your feelings since they were battling themselves? Since they were egotistically centered around their requirements? Or on the other hand, since they didn't realize that feelings matter? Was your Disregard dynamic or latent, gutless or harmless? How could it influence you as a kid, and how can it influence you now? Understanding your CEN on a profound level will liberate you from self-fault and disgrace, and approve your experience.

2. Acknowledge that your feelings are closed off, yet they are still there, sitting tight for you.

Your kid's cerebrum safeguarded you by walling off your feelings, however, it couldn't make them disappear totally. Today you can in any case get to them. By tolerating that they exist, you'll have the option to figure out how to pay attention to them, use them and oversee them.

3. Focus on your sentiments.

This is likely the absolute most remarkable thing you can do to adapt to your CEN. It's a method for doing something contrary to what your folks showed you, begin to respect your sentiments, and arrive across the wall to the wealth, variety, and association that lies on the opposite side: your feelings. Focusing on your sentiments will permit you to start to involve them as they are intended to be utilized.

4. Practice sitting with gloomy sentiments to build your resistance.

Figuring out how to sit areas of strength with agonizing sentiments is one of the early structure blocks to realizing all of the feeling abilities. Sitting with gloomy sentiments will place you in charge of yourself.

5. Keep a continuous rundown of your Preferences.

Focus and accept extraordinary notes as you go as the day progressed. Record all that you can find that you either do or could do without. It tends to be little, medium, or huge, however, nothing is excessively little to make the rundown. Knowing these things about yourself can position you to make yourself more joyful.

6. Create and rehearse empathy for yourself.

As an individual with CEN, you are likely far kinder to others than you are to yourself. Attempt to acknowledge that as a person, you have the very privileges that you permit every other person. You will commit errors, you will settle on unfortunate choices, and you will fizzle. What's more, you ought not to be any crueler on yourself for those things than you would be on a companion who you love. Rehearsing self-sympathy will assemble your confidence.

7. Become mindful of the sensation of outrage when it occurs in your body.

Of the multitude of feelings, outrage is the one that, when closed off rather than communicated and made due, will consume you. Becoming mindful of your resentment will quickly begin to calm and enable you.

8. Peruse a book on self-assuredness.

Figuring out how to be self-assured is the partner to becoming mindful of your annoyance. Being decisive is a method for getting others to hear what you feel, hear and require. Learning decisiveness will make others esteem you more.

9. Share your CEN story with somebody near you.

There is something about sharing your CEN story that permits you to truly possess it and take it. Informing somebody regarding your CEN will assist you with feeling less troubled and alone.

10 Search for the impacts of CEN on your essential connections.

Has your Young life Close to home Disregarded worked out in your marriage? Impacted how you've nurtured your kids? Caused you to feel awkward with your folks? Searching for the impacts of CEN in your connections will make the way for your loved ones.

Chapter 6

Step-by-step instructions to pardon your dad for genuinely Absent

"The greatest example I have learned in life about my resentment towards my dad is: The more annoyance towards the past that I convey in my heart, the less competent I am of adoring in the present," says Braswell. "It is fundamental that illegitimate children are upheld in more than one way to address our aggravation and outrage suitably so we can be positive male good examples for all kids."

Braswell needs to assist with peopling managing the aggravation and outrage they feel. He offers these useful tidbits to those growing up without their dad:

Recognize the indignation. Numerous guys set forth an extreme outside, yet within the outrage is seething. Recognize it.

Embrace pardoning. It takes a resilient individual to pardon somebody they don't feel merits their pardoning. At the point when you don't excuse yourself, you permit agony to live in your heart. Pardoning provides the advantage of understanding and a sense of finality.

Embrace your heart. At the point when you embrace your heart, you need to deliver anything that causes torment. The best way to do that is through affection. You can't do it through disdain.

Impart through straightforwardness. You need to figure out how to impart your sentiments, not simply express them. A ton of what bastard folks manage is a consequence of not having any desire to discuss what's going on within. This truly isn't about the other individual, it is about you delivering yourself to develop.

"I want to be a positive good example for my child and different youngsters," Braswell says. "Once in a while, I felt like I needed to tell the world I was alright. Also, my dad was irrelevant in my life to stifle the way that his nonappearance was very huge in my life.

"I will always be unable to offer the world my best in light of the disdain of another. Particularly not the contempt of my dad."

On the off chance that you're thinking about pardoning, ever, congratulations. The way that you would try and ponder showing elegance, love, and benevolence toward somebody who's treated you is an indication that you have incredible compassion and strength. It very well may be incredibly hard to pardon somebody, particularly assuming how they treated you had enduring repercussions, and that is unquestionably the situation when we're deserted by the individual who should adore and uphold us regardless of anything else. So once more, on the off chance that you're perusing this since you're pondering pardoning a parent who left you, pause for a minute to be pleased with yourself. Presently, we should discuss pardoning.

How To Pardon a Parent Who Left You When You Were Youthful?

Indeed, you've likely heard this maxim previously, however here it is once more, since it's simply, honestly, valid: Pardoning is more for you than it is for the other individual. It's tied in with lifting the weight of that aggravation from your heart so you have the profound investment for other more blissful things. There's no need to focus on disregarding some unacceptable that has been finished or discrediting the aggravation you've felt, yet it is tied in with accounting for something better in your future by getting the past into the rear of your brain where it can go lethargic.

Reasons (Not Reasons) For Deserting

The primary spot to begin with regards to absolution is sympathy, and as we've proactively laid out, you're associated with your compassion just by the excellence of thinking about this demonstration of pardoning. Also, what's sympathy? It's putting yourself in the other individual's shoes for one minute and giving a valiant effort to figure out the contemplations and sentiments that prompted their choices. On the off chance that you can essentially attempt to comprehend where your parent was coming from when they went with the choice to leave you, then, at that point, you could see a way to pardoning.